# A LIFE IN THE DAY OF BILL THE FLY

# A LIFE IN THE DAY OF BILL THE FLY

## JC QUINTANA

Copyright © 2024 by JC Quintana

All rights reserved. No part of this book may be reproduced in any manner whatsoever without written permission except in the case of brief quotations embodied in critical articles and reviews.

First Printing, 2024

# Bill the Fly

# 1

# Into My Life, Into My Day

The world sparkled with morning dew as Bill the Fly buzzed to life, stretching his wings for the very first time. The warm sunlight shone upon him like a giant blanket, and he felt a sudden thrill—a sense that something special was about to happen. He hovered above the pond, taking in the vastness of this strange new world. The shimmering water stretched far and wide, dotted with lily pads and surrounded by tall reeds that swayed gently in the breeze.

As Bill flitted around, another newly born fly buzzed up beside him. The fly had a concerned, frightened look in his tiny, multifaceted eyes.

"Good morning, fellow new fly," the fly greeted him with a nervous smile. "Enjoying your first day?"

Bill buzzed with excitement. "Oh yes! It's amazing! There's so much to see and explore. I feel like I could fly forever!"

The other fly's smile softened further. "Ah, I want to feel the excitement. But remember, we flies don't have much time. In fact, we only have one day."

Bill's wings stilled, and he stared at the other fly. "One day?" he echoed, a shiver running down his tiny body.

"Yes," the other fly replied, his tone nervous and serious. "We have to make the most of the time we're given."

Bill's heart fluttered. Only one day? How could anyone possibly fit all of life into such a short span? As he thought about it, a new feeling rose in him—not fear, but determination. If he only had one day, then he would make it the best day anyone had ever had. He would learn all he could and meet as many creatures as possible. Surely, there was much more to life than just buzzing about.

"Then I'll make every second count!" Bill declared, his wings buzzing with new fly energy.

With a nod, the other fly slowly drifted away. "Good luck to you, but I am staying here where it is safe!" he called over his shoulder. "The world is scary and dangerous with so much to worry about."

Bill took a deep breath and surveyed the pond, which was now bustling with life. Birds chirped from the trees, frogs croaked from the lily pads, and the gentle ripples of the water hinted at mysteries below the surface. Where should he go first? What should he do with his precious time?

# Brock the Crock

# 2

# Meeting Brock the Croc

Just then, he spotted a long, sleek figure lying on a sun-warmed log by the pond's edge. It was Brock the Crocodile, his eyes half-closed as he soaked in the morning sun. Although only a few minutes old, Bill had heard stories about crocodiles—they were fierce and mighty, and many animals feared them. But Brock the croc looked so peaceful that Bill felt strangely drawn to him.

With a burst of confidence, Bill flew over to the large crocodile. He wanted to know what wisdom this grand creature might hold.

"Excuse me, Mr. Crocodile!" Bill buzzed as he hovered in the air above Brock's long, toothy snout. "I'm Bill, and I've just started my one and only day. I want to know how to make the most of it. Do you have any advice?"

Brock opened one eye and gave a slow, toothy grin. "Well, well, Bill. It's not often that a fly comes to chat with me," he rumbled in a deep, slow voice. "So, you want to make the most of your day, do you? Come closer, and I'll tell you a little something about generosity."

Bill settled onto the edge of the log, ready to listen closely.

Bill perched on the sun-warmed log, his wings tucked neatly behind him as he gazed up at Brock the Crocodile. Brock's leathery skin gleamed in the sunlight, and his broad, powerful tail lay curled at his side. The massive crocodile looked like he could snap up a dozen flies without a second thought, but his calm demeanor made Bill feel safe enough to stay.

"So, little fly," Brock began, his deep voice vibrating through the log, "you want to make the most of your day? That's a good thought. You know, I may seem like a big, fearsome creature, but I've learned something important about giving back."

Bill's tiny eyes sparkled with curiosity. "Giving back? But, Mr. Crocodile, you're so strong. Don't you just take what you need?"

Brock let out a rumbling chuckle. "You'd think so, wouldn't you? But I've found that the happiest moments in life come not from taking, but from giving. You see, Bill, there was a time when I didn't think much about others. I'd go about my day, snapping up fish and frogs, thinking that was all there was to life. But one day, something changed."

Bill buzzed with interest, settling in as Brock continued his story.

"It was a day much like this one," Brock began, gazing into the distance as if he were watching the scene unfold again. "I was lounging here by the pond when I noticed a little frog trapped in a patch of reeds. He was struggling, poor thing, and I could see he wasn't going to make it out on his own."

Bill leaned forward, hanging on Brock's every word.

"I could've ignored him," Brock admitted, his voice a bit softer now. "I could've just left him there and gone about my business. But something about that little frog's struggle touched me. So, I reached over and gently nudged him free. The little fellow was so grateful, he started telling all the other animals how I'd helped him. For the first time, Bill, I felt something more satisfying than a full belly. I felt joy."

Bill's wings buzzed with excitement. "Wow, Mr. Crocodile, that's amazing! But aren't you supposed to be the king of the pond? Isn't that enough?"

Brock shook his massive head slowly. "Being the strongest doesn't mean much if you have no one to share it with. Since that day, I've made it a point to help where I can. I've even given some fish a safe place to hide from predators now and then. And you know what? Every time I do something for someone else, I feel that same joy all over again. It's like I'm making my day just a little bit brighter."

Bill was quiet for a moment, letting Brock's words sink in. "So, being generous isn't just about what you give away. It's about what you feel inside?"

"Exactly, little one," Brock replied with a slow blink. "When you give, you get something far more precious than anything you could take. You get a joy that stays with you, a happiness that fills you up from the inside out. And that, I think, is what makes life worthwhile."

Bill's wings fluttered with a new excitement. He'd thought being a fly meant just taking whatever he could find before the day ended. But now, he realized that there was something even better he could do with his time. He could give back, just like Brock.

"Thank you, Mr. Crocodile," Bill said, his voice full of awe. "I think I understand now. I want to share my day with others, too!"

Brock nodded approvingly, a gentle smile playing on his scaly face. "Good lad. You're on the right path. And remember, generosity doesn't always mean big things. Sometimes, it's the little acts of kindness that make the biggest difference."

Bill thanked Brock once more and prepared to continue his journey. As he fluttered away from the log, he felt lighter than ever, as if Brock's words had filled his tiny body with a glowing warmth. He knew there was more to learn and more animals to meet, but now he had a purpose: to share his day in a way that would bring joy to others.

Ahead, he spotted the familiar slow, steady movements of Mertle the Turtle along the pond's edge. Intrigued, Bill buzzed toward her, eager to see what more he could learn on his one and only day.

# Mertle the Turtle

# 3

# A Talk with Mertle the Turtle

Bill flitted above the pond, his heart still warm from Brock the Crocodile's story of generosity. He felt a new sense of purpose filling him up, guiding his wings as he searched for his next encounter. It wasn't long before he spotted Mertle the Turtle slowly making her way along the edge of the pond, her shell glistening in the sun, and her head bobbing gently with each step.

Bill hovered down to greet her, landing lightly on a nearby reed. "Hello, Ms. Turtle!" he chirped. "My name's Bill, and I'm trying to make the most of my day. Mr. Crocodile told me about generosity, and now I'm wondering if you have any advice on how I can spend my time well."

Mertle the Turtle blinked slowly and turned her head to peer at Bill. "Well now, young fly, it's not often I get visitors who want to listen to an old turtle like me," she said with a soft smile. "But if you're looking for advice, I'd be happy to share a bit of what I've learned. You see, I believe that self-control is one of the most precious things we can practice."

"Self-control?" Bill asked, tilting his head. "What do you mean?"

Mertle smiled knowingly and paused to take a slow, deep breath. "I've seen a lot in my time here by the pond, Bill. You might say I've been around for a while. And one thing I've noticed is that those who rush and let their feelings take over often end up in trouble."

Bill's wings fluttered with curiosity as he listened.

"I used to be quite a hasty turtle," Mertle continued, with a hint of nostalgia in her voice. "When I was younger, I'd dart around as quickly as my legs could carry me. I'd get flustered, frustrated, and upset whenever something didn't go my way. But over time, I realized that by slowing down and learning to control my reactions, I could see things more clearly."

Bill pondered this. "But isn't it hard to go slow all the time? I feel like there's so much to see and do!"

"Ah, that's exactly why self-control is so important, Bill," Mertle replied. "When we master our emotions and take our time, we can think more clearly and help others better. When we rush and let our feelings take over, we often end up hurting ourselves or others without even realizing it."

She took another steadying breath, then continued. "For example, if I get angry when the fish swim by too fast and splash water on me, I could yell at them, or I could take a deep breath, let it go, and remember that they're just having fun. It's the same with fear or sadness. When you let these feelings control you, you miss out on the good things happening around you."

Bill looked around at the peaceful pond, realizing how calm it made him feel just being near it. "So, if I practice self-control, I'll have more time to enjoy what's around me?"

"Exactly, Bill," Mertle said, her eyes twinkling with warmth. "And more importantly, you'll have more time to help others. When you're calm and in control, you're able to be there for your friends when they need you."

Bill felt a rush of understanding, as if a new light had been switched on in his mind. "Thank you, Ms. Turtle," he said, buzzing excitedly. "I think I understand now. When I feel rushed or worried, I'll try to take a deep breath and slow down. That way, I can enjoy my day more and be there for others too."

Mertle nodded slowly. "You're a quick learner, Bill. Just remember, life may be short, but with self-control, you can make every moment count."

Bill thanked Mertle and fluttered up to get a better view of the pond. He saw the glimmer of fish scales near the surface, where Mitch the Fish was darting around with his friends. Eager to continue his journey and put Mertle's advice into practice, Bill buzzed down toward the water to greet Mitch.

# Mitch the Fish

# 4

# The Kindness of Mitch the Fish

Bill buzzed with anticipation as he flitted over the pond, making his way toward the glistening water where Mitch the Fish was playfully darting about. Mitch was sleek and shiny, his scales reflecting the sunlight in a dazzling display of colors. Bill could see him swimming in circles, occasionally breaking the surface with a splash as he chased his fish friends through the water.

Bill hovered over the water and called out, "Hello, Mitch! My name's Bill, and I'm learning how to make the most of my one and only day. I've already spoken to Brock the Crocodile and Mertle the Turtle, and they've taught me about generosity and self-control. Do you have any advice on how I can spend my day well?"

Mitch swam closer and paused, his curious eyes sparkling as he looked up at Bill. "Well, hello there, Bill! I'd be happy to share a bit of advice," he replied in a cheerful, gurgly voice. "If you ask me, kindness is one of the best things you can share with others. It's something that makes life brighter for everyone, even us fish."

Bill tilted his head. "Kindness? How can being kind help me make the most of my day?"

Mitch flicked his tail and began swimming lazily in a circle. "Let me tell you a little story. Not too long ago, I met a lonely minnow named Max. Poor Max didn't have any friends, and he was too shy to join our group. At first, I didn't think much of it—I was busy having fun with my own friends. But then, I decided to invite him to swim with us."

Bill leaned forward, listening intently as Mitch continued.

"At first, Max was nervous, but I kept encouraging him. I told him he was welcome to join us anytime. Slowly, he started to open up, and soon enough, he was swimming and playing along with the rest of us. You should've seen the smile on his face! And you know what? Seeing him happy made me feel happy, too."

Bill buzzed with excitement. "That's amazing, Mitch! So, by being kind, you helped Max and yourself feel good?"

"Exactly," Mitch replied, flicking his tail playfully. "Kindness isn't just a gift to others; it's a gift to yourself, too. When you're kind, you feel a warmth inside that's hard to find anywhere else. And the best part? It doesn't cost a thing. Kindness is something you can give all day long, to everyone you meet."

Bill thought about this, imagining how much joy he could spread just by being kind to others. "But what if I don't have much time to show kindness to everyone I meet?" he asked, his voice tinged with worry.

Mitch smiled, his eyes crinkling at the edges. "Oh, Bill, kindness doesn't have to take much time at all. Sometimes, it's as simple as a friendly smile or a few kind words. Even just being patient with others can make a big difference. When you're kind, you're planting seeds that grow into happy memories—not just for others, but for yourself as well."

Bill felt a rush of excitement as he imagined all the little acts of kindness he could share throughout the day. He remembered Brock's lesson about generosity and Mertle's advice on self-control, and he realized that kindness was another piece of the puzzle he needed to complete his day.

"Thank you, Mitch," Bill said, his voice filled with gratitude. "I think I understand now. Kindness isn't just about making others happy; it's about creating a life filled with warmth and joy."

Mitch gave a cheerful flip of his fin. "You've got it, Bill! And remember, being kind to yourself is just as important. Sometimes, we're hardest on ourselves, but if you take a moment to be gentle with yourself, you'll find life is a lot sweeter."

With a wave of his tail, Mitch dove back into the water, joining his friends in another playful swim. Bill watched him go, his heart full of warmth and new purpose. He was beginning to see how each lesson fit together, forming a beautiful picture of how to live a full and happy life.

Bill's gaze wandered along the pond's edge until he spotted Gail the Snail slowly inching her way up a tall blade of grass. Inspired by the kindness he'd just learned about, Bill buzzed over to Gail, eager to discover what wisdom she might have to share.

# Gail the Snail

# 5

# Mindful Gail the Snail

As Bill buzzed along the pond's edge, he caught sight of Gail the Snail inching her way up a tall, dewy blade of grass. She moved with such deliberation, each tiny step a careful journey on its own. Bill was fascinated by her slow pace, so different from the frantic energy he often felt inside.

"Hello, Ms. Snail!" Bill greeted her, landing on a nearby leaf to watch her as she moved.

Gail turned her head slowly, her eyes swiveling to focus on the little fly before her. "Well, hello there, young one," she said with a gentle smile. "What brings you to this part of the pond?"

"I'm Bill, and I'm trying to make the most of my one day," he explained. "I've learned about generosity, self-control, and kindness, but I still want to know more. Everyone seems to have some wisdom to share, so I thought I'd see if you do, too."

Gail gave a slow, thoughtful nod. "Oh, indeed I do. I believe in taking things slow and savoring each moment. Life is precious, you see, and there's so much beauty to enjoy if you just take the time to look."

Bill's wings buzzed with curiosity. "But I only have one day! If I go too slowly, won't I miss out on everything?"

Gail chuckled softly, a sound as light as the rustling of leaves. "Ah, but if you rush, you might miss the most important things of all. You see, Bill, moving slowly doesn't mean missing out. Quite the opposite! When you take your time, you can truly see the world around you. You notice the colors of the flowers, the warmth of the sun, and the scent of the fresh, damp earth."

Bill looked around, and for the first time, he took a deep breath and really saw the world. He noticed the gentle ripples in the pond, the vibrant green of the leaves, and the tiny droplets of dew glistening in the sunlight like little jewels.

Gail continued, "Sometimes, we're in such a hurry that we forget to enjoy what's right in front of us. I may move slowly, but that means I get to see the things others miss. I watch the grass grow, I hear the birds sing, and I feel the cool shade when I pass under a tree. Every step is a chance to savor something new."

Bill marveled at this idea. He'd never thought about it that way before. He was always zipping around, feeling like he had to hurry to fit everything in. But now, he wondered if slowing down might actually allow him to experience more.

"But what if I want to see everything?" he asked. "I feel like there's so much I need to do."

Gail smiled kindly. "Oh, Bill, it's not about seeing everything. It's about seeing what matters most. You can't be everywhere at once, but you can be right here, right now, fully present in this moment. By savoring each experience, you're not just living—you're truly appreciating the life you have."

Bill thought about the moments he'd shared with Brock, Mertle, and Mitch. Each of them had taught him something different, and he realized that he might have missed these lessons if he'd rushed through his day without stopping to really listen.

"Thank you, Ms. Snail," Bill said, his voice filled with newfound understanding. "I think I understand now. Slowing down doesn't mean missing out—it means I get to enjoy each moment to the fullest."

Gail nodded, her eyes warm and wise. "That's right, Bill. Life may be short, but when you savor each moment, it feels full and rich. Take your time. Enjoy the sunshine, the colors, the sounds. Let your heart fill with the beauty around you."

Bill felt a peacefulness settle over him as he took in Gail's words. He looked around the pond with fresh eyes, noticing details he hadn't seen before—the way the sunlight danced on the water, the soft rustle of the reeds, the distant song of a bird high above. Everything seemed more vibrant, more alive.

As he said goodbye to Gail, Bill felt a gentle gratitude for the moments he'd spent with each friend. He now understood that his day wasn't just about rushing to see and do everything—it was about truly being present for each experience, no matter how big or small.

With this new sense of calm and purpose, Bill fluttered off, ready to reflect on all he'd learned. He found a quiet spot by the pond's edge, where he could ponder the lessons from his friends and discover what they all meant for him.

# Reflecting by the Pond

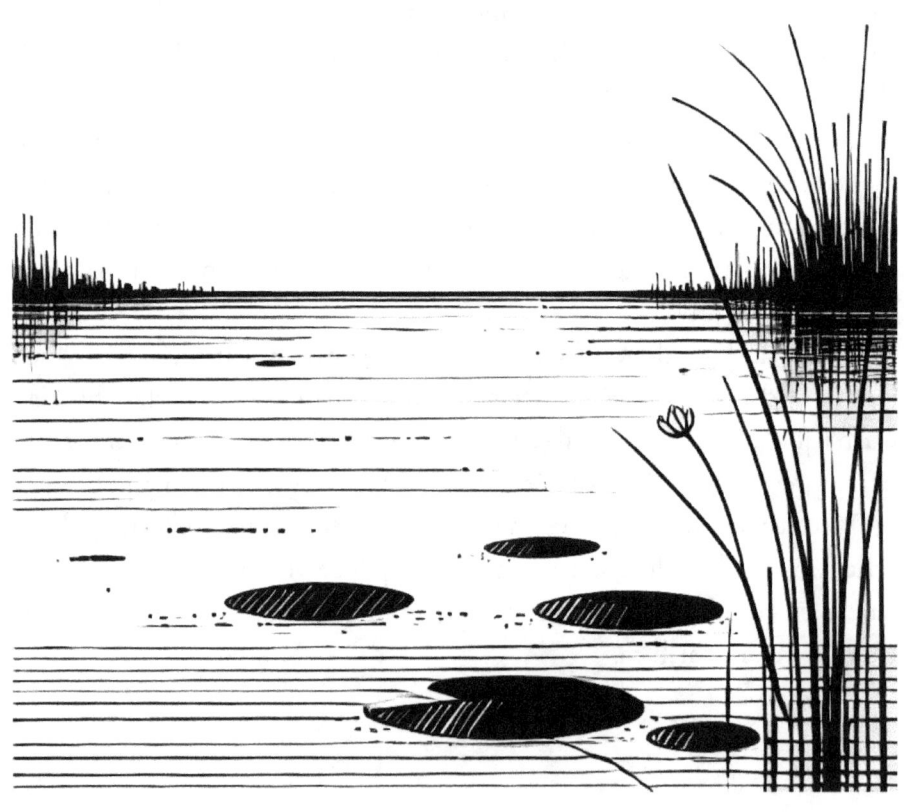

# 6

# Reflecting on a Day Well Lived

As the sun began its slow descent behind the trees, again casting a tender, golden glow over the pond, Bill found a peaceful spot on a broad, flat leaf to rest. He had spent the day buzzing from one new friend to another, gathering pieces of wisdom like the droplets of dew he had first seen following his birth. Now, he felt full, not just of knowledge, but of a deep, satisfying goodness that made his heart feel bigger than ever.

Bill gazed out over the pond, his mind swirling with thoughts of all the wonderful creatures he'd met. Brock the Croc, who had taught him about generosity. Brock's story of helping the little frog showed Bill that true joy comes from giving to others and that every small act of kindness can ripple outward, like the gentle waves on the pond.

Mertle the Turtle, who had shown him the power of self-control. Her calm and steady way of moving through the world reminded Bill that sometimes, the best way to make a difference is to take a deep breath and think before acting. With self-control, he could be a better friend to others and could help them with their own struggles.

Mitch the Fish, who had spoken of kindness. Mitch's story about befriending the lonely minnow touched Bill's heart. Kindness, Mitch had explained, wasn't just for others—it was also a gift to oneself. Bill realized that he wanted to live his day with a heart full of kindness, both for his friends and for himself.

Finally, there was Gail the Snail, whose slow and thoughtful pace showed Bill the beauty of savoring each moment. She had taught him that by taking his time, he could see and feel more of the world around him. Bill now understood that life wasn't just about rushing from one thing to the next, but about truly being present for the things that mattered most.

As he sat there, letting all of these thoughts settle into his heart, Bill felt a gentle breeze ripple through the reeds. He closed his eyes, listening to the sounds of the pond—the soft croak of a distant frog, the rustle of leaves, the quiet hum of other insects going about their day. Everything felt connected, as if each creature, each lesson, was a piece of a larger, beautiful puzzle.

Bill opened his eyes and took another look around. His day was drawing to a close, but instead of feeling sad, he felt content. He had met wonderful friends, learned valuable lessons, and found a sense of peace he hadn't known when the day began. Most of all, he had learned that living a good life didn't require more time—it required a big heart, open eyes, and the willingness to embrace every moment with love.

He thought about the joy that Brock had spoken of, the calm that Mertle had embodied, the kindness Mitch had shared, and the mindfulness that Gail had shown. It all came together in a single, beautiful realization: living fully means living with love, no matter how short the time might be.

Bill took a deep breath, letting the air fill him up one last time. He felt grateful for every moment, every friend, every lesson. He had truly made the most of his day, and in doing so, he had discovered that life, no matter how short, was worth living.

As the first stars began to twinkle in the evening sky, Bill closed his eyes, feeling a peaceful satisfaction settle over him. His day had been filled with joy, reflection, and connection, and he knew that he had lived it well.

# Life is What You Make It

# 7

# What a Great Day, What a Great Flight

As the night began to blanket the pond in a soft, silvery glow, Bill opened his eyes and took in the world around him one last time. The stars were beginning to peek out, dotting the sky like tiny fireflies, and the air had a cool, gentle stillness that made everything feel just a little bit more magical.

He had learned so much in his one short day, met friends who had changed him forever, and found joy in ways he had never expected. His heart was full of love for the pond, for the creatures who called it home, and for the life he had lived.

He stretched his wings and rose slowly into the air, savoring the feeling of the breeze against his tiny body. He flew over the pond, gliding above the rippling water and past the tall reeds, now casting long shadows in the moonlight. As he drifted by, he caught sight of Brock the Crocodile resting on his favorite log, his eyes closed in peaceful slumber. Bill felt a warm glow of gratitude for Brock's wisdom and the joy that generosity had brought him.

Bill passed Mertle the Turtle, who was tucked into her shell by the water's edge. Her calm presence reminded him to take each moment as it came, with patience and self-control. Next, he spotted Mitch the Fish, who leapt out of the water in a playful splash, his scales reflecting the silvery light of the moon. Mitch's kindness had shown Bill how even the smallest acts could make a world of difference.

Finally, Bill drifted over the blade of grass where he'd last seen Gail the Snail. She was still there, her shell glistening in the starlight, her slow and steady presence a reminder to savor every moment. Bill felt a profound peace settle over him as he realized how each of these friends had become a part of him. They had filled his day with wisdom, kindness, and love, and he carried their lessons with him now, like tiny treasures tucked inside his heart.

Bill took one last flight around the pond, tracing a graceful arc through the night air. He watched the moonlight dance on the water and felt the gentle whisper of the breeze against his wings. Everything was perfect, just as it was, and he knew that he had lived his day as fully as any fly could hope to.

As he glided back to the quiet spot on the leaf, Bill felt a gentle sense of completion. His day had been filled with meaning and purpose, and he felt ready to rest, his heart full of gratitude for the beautiful life he had been given.

He closed his eyes and let the peacefulness of the night settle over him like a soft blanket. With a final, contented sigh, Bill drifted off, knowing that he had embraced every moment, every lesson, and every friend. He had truly discovered what it meant to live a good life.

And as the stars twinkled overhead, the pond grew quiet, holding within it the memory of a tiny fly who had, in one short day, discovered the true beauty of living fully.

# 8

# The Flight of Bill the Fly

In the light of dawn, Bill awoke,
With wings that fluttered as he spoke,
"One day I have to see it all,
Before the night and shadows fall."
 To Brock the Croc, so wise and grand,
Bill flew with heart and open hand.
"Generosity," the croc did say,
"Brings joy that never fades away."
 Then Mertle Turtle, slow and wise,
Taught Bill to see through patient eyes,
"With self-control, you'll find the way,
To help a friend on any day."
 And Mitch the Fish, so bright and kind,
Showed Bill the gift that hearts can find,
"When kindness flows from deep within,
It's warmth and joy that truly win."
 Last came Gail, so calm and still,
She taught him how to truly feel,

"To savor time, slow down, take care,
For life is precious everywhere."
    So Bill took flight as evening fell,
With heart so full, no words could tell,
The peace he found in every friend,
The joy that bloomed from start to end.
    With wings aglow in silver light,
He soared into the star-filled night,
For in one day, he'd come to see,
The beauty in life's brevity.

www.ingramcontent.com/pod-product-compliance
Lightning Source LLC
Chambersburg PA
CBHW052309300426
44110CB00035B/2311